Dear Val,

For my "final" reader.

GOT IT!

Your thoughtful comments and keen eye helped

Twenty-One
Communication Tips
for
Busy, Impatient People

me so much. Enjoy the finished product!

by

Joan Craven

Joan :)

STRATEGIC BOOK GROUP

Strategic Book Group
P.O. Box 333
Durham CT 06422
www.StrategicBookClub.com

ISBN: 978-1-60976-690-0

Printed in the United States of America

Book Design: Bonita S. Watson

Praise For *Got It!*

"Joan Craven demonstrates her mastery of communications by weaving theory, experience, and thought-provoking questions into a quick and easy read that is a practical guide to effective communications principles. If you want to improve communication skills for yourself, your family, or your team, you must get *Got It*!"

—Don Boynton, Executive Director, Corporate Communication, Travel Alberta, Canada

"If you are seeking simple, pragmatic tips to improve your effectiveness through better communications and management skills, then this book is for you! It's quick to read and easy to remember."

—Sarah Raiss, Executive Vice-President of Corporate Services, TransCanada Corporation, Canada

"At a time when the ways we communicate are changing so rapidly, there are some incredibly simple yet pertinent tactics here that will save stress and frustration. Despite these changes in speed and method of communication, the basic principles remain the same and the next generation of leaders would do well to be reminded of them."

**—Gordon Ritchie, Vice Chairman,
RBC Capital Markets, Canada**

"*Got It!* could aptly be renamed the *Little Book of Hundreds of Useful Ideas!* This is a book that should be at the side of the desk and reflected on often by busy executives, students, or anyone who simply wants to improve their verbal or written communication skills. It's full of constructive ideas and common sense guidelines for improving what each of us does every day. It's the best two hours of reading I have spent in a long time."

**—Monty Carter, Senior Vice President Sales,
Enterprise Solutions, TELUS, Canada**

"Joan Craven brings a practical and thoughtful approach to the communication opportunities and challenges that senior leaders encounter daily. Joan's wealth of experience is demonstrated by the clear and direct strategies that will empower and enable us all to be more effective communicators and leaders."

**—Don Hoium, Director of Education,
Regina Public Schools, Canada**

"Joan's honest, insightful words give me hope that through thoughtful communications, the quality of my relationships will improve. Her easy-to-incorporate techniques are clearly articulated and make sense. Readers will feel supported and optimistic that they will improve their communication skills."

**—Ruth Ridgeway, Training Coordinator,
Insights Vacations, England**

"Sincere and respectful communication in the workplace is something I strongly believe in, and the techniques discussed in this book will definitely help develop that kind of culture. In particular, the advice on handling difficult conversations will be useful to both new and experienced managers. The book provides many useful tips for a manager's toolbox."

"*Got It!* is filled with thought-provoking ideas to help you communicate with anyone in a caring, honest manner without compromising your values. Joan's compassionate voice resonates throughout."

Dedications

In loving memory of my dear friend, Nancy Hole Charland, who taught me the difference between what matters and what does not.

To my husband Bob, in gratitude for his unwavering belief that whatever I do in life makes a positive difference in people's lives. His steadfast support of all my careers and roles gives me strength.

Contents

Chapter 1   Trust Is A Must: Honest Conversations Make A
             Difference. 1
Chapter 2   Extreme Words. 5
Chapter 3   Email Blues 9
Chapter 4   Silence Opens Doors 13
Chapter 5   Do One Thing Well 17
Chapter 6   Are You Giving Piano Lessons?
             We've Got To Start Meeting Like This 21
Chapter 7   Cut Yourself Off. 25
Chapter 8   Key Messages 28
Chapter 9   Nip It In The "But" 33
Chapter 10   Back To The Future 37
Chapter 11   Lower The Bar. 41
Chapter 12   Anti-Jekyll And Hyde 45
Chapter 13   Drain, Drain, Go Away 49

Chapter 14   Authentic People 54

Chapter 15   Trust Your Gut 59

Chapter 16   Do It Now: Nike Is Right. 63

Chapter 17   Dissonant Values And
                       Workplace Stress 67

Chapter 18   Any Void In Information Leads to
                       Miscommunication 71

Chapter 19   Take A Break! 75

Chapter 20   Box Up Your Worries. 80

Chapter 21   Quit Complaining: Your Problems
                       Will Diminish. 84

Introduction

Usually when we run into difficulties, both professional and personal, all crumbs lead back to poor communication. It might relate back to our body language, our choice of words, or the way we reacted to the words and the other person's body language.

When asked if the person who is upsetting you has been told, the answer is often, "Yes, in my head." We won't risk an honest conversation and yet we let something someone has said or done upset us sometimes for years. This is not good for our mental or physical health.

When my godson was three, I asked him to finish off his milk before he began his dessert. He put his little arms on his hips and said, "Auntie Joan, I am the boss of myself!" You know, he was correct. He could make the choice . . . and then he would live with the consequences.

As adults, we, too, are the boss of ourselves. We can be angry or upset, or we can decide to build a bridge and get over it. Will it matter in five hours, five months, or five years? If not, start building. If it will matter, do something.

The older I get, the more I realize that there are key principles to remember in communication. Think before you speak, be thoughtfully honest, and speak to others as you would a very dear friend. You will become much happier, professionally and personally.

Over the past few years, I have interviewed and observed thousands of people. The information they have given me has helped me compile the practical communication tips found in this book. I hope you won't just read the chapters; I would like you to take time to truthfully and thoughtfully answer the questions at the end of each one.

At first read, you may think I'm advocating that you become a pushover; that's not true. What I'm asking you to do is to take responsibility for your communication.

It's been my observation that, at the end of our lives, it really doesn't matter whether we have lots of things, have travelled the world, or have been what others might think of as an important person; what we will care about is the memories others will have of us. What is the great secret to creating fond memories? That's easy, and only you have the power to do it: be thoughtful in all your communications.

Chapter 1

Trust Is a Must:
Honest Conversations Make A Difference

I'm often asked, "So, what does a communication consultant do?" At first, I struggled with the answer because it's a little of this and a little of that. One day, however, it became clear. Three simple words: "I build relationships."

Relationships must be built on trust, honesty, and openness. A lasting relationship is developed through good communication techniques, whether it is between a spokesperson and the media, a company and its consumers, leaders and their staff, or between life partners. Honest, caring communication builds trust.

Early on in our marriage, my husband came home and said that he and a group of colleagues were chatting about what it was like being married. As he listened, it soon became clear that many of them were struggling with trying to understand what was on their partners' minds.

My husband looked at me and said, "That's never been our problem; you tell me exactly what you are thinking!" That's true. It only makes good sense to share the truth with a person with whom you want to build a long-term relationship. If you can't be truthful, at work or at home, you are doomed to failure.

There are so many things that can go wrong in any relationship and most point back to a miscommunication. When you expect the other person to be a mind reader, you are setting up that relationship for failure. If you can't speak your mind, how can any relationship move forward?

Honest Conversations Make The Difference

I have observed at some business meetings that people all nod in agreement, like trained seals, and never voice an opinion. Other places, there are lively discussions and lots of sharing of rich ideas. What is the difference?

In the productive meetings, trust had been built and caring honesty was valued. People were heard, their opinions valued, and no one came in with a preplanned agenda. At the conclusion, decisions were made based on everyone's input. While that particular decision might not be one that some members wanted, they agreed because everyone's input had been considered. They knew that their contributions were valued and that the conclusions were in the best interests of the team.

In meetings where people had the trained-seal mentality and they were simply rubber-stamping the leader, openness wasn't valued. Long-term employees knew that the leader had already made up her mind and just wanted to give the illusion of collaboration. I always thought the term *clobbering*, rather than *collaborating* was more appropriate. Long-term employees had come to realize that their input only slowed down the worthless process.

It didn't take long for new team members, bursting with energy and ideas, to retreat and clap their flippers at the leader's latest idea. How sad.

Test Your Honesty

Examine the conversations you have with others. If you are in a leadership position, are you leading a group of trained seals, or do you have a team that feels empowered to bring all its expertise to the table? If your team resembles seals, start to listen more and talk less.

Are you asking those around you to be mind readers and to figure out what you think? If you are, you are heading for potential conflicts.

When you constantly tell the truth and give honest opinions, you are taking the first steps in building a relationship. Thoughtful honesty won't hurt when the person realizes you care and want to make things better. The silent treatment does not work and over time creates mountains out of molehills.

When people are not free to speak their mind and you do not share your honest opinion, they begin to give up. While honest communication isn't always the easiest – and it will take more time at the beginning – it is the only way to build a long-term, trusting relationship.

Got It?

1. What do people say are the three things they need to know in order to get along with you?

     a.

     b.

     c.

2. Are you holding things in and having difficult conversations with everyone but the person who really needs to hear? Then make a commitment to change that now.

     I will have a conversation with _____ on _____ _____ (add the date)

Chapter 2

Extreme Words

What happened to face-to-face communication? What about sticking to the facts? My leadership team and I once wasted valuable time trying to decide what to do about staff exceeding their coffee-breaks. After about 10 minutes, the newest member of the team cautiously asked, "Why not time the break one of the people takes and when he returns, if it is longer than the recommended 15 minutes, talk to him about it?"

What? Confront the offenders directly? Why not? We certainly did not need to waste everyone's time on a problem that was only affecting a small group. Or was it?

The other point this new "leader" made was to time the break so we had facts, not inferences. Perhaps we imagined that the breaks were getting longer when, in fact, they were within company guidelines.

Often we start to think something is much larger than it is when we have no facts to back up our perception. It was time to make some observations and to rely on facts instead of our impressions.

Awfulizing Situations

We also do this with our self-talk. By exaggerating and using extreme words, we work ourselves up. Don't let that annoying little voice in your head say, "You never; You always; This is the worst; It is terrible." Instead, ask yourself, "Is it true?" and "What is true?" When you describe what has happened, with no embellishments, you will usually bring the situation down to size.

The minute we think, "Everyone is doing it," (or "not doing it"), we get into trouble and fall into a very deep blame/shame hole. Instead, ask yourself, "Is this true?" and "What is true?" and then make some solid go-forward plans based on "just the facts, ma'am."

When you do decide to comment on a behaviour you would liked changed, do so in a caring, factual manner. Your comments should only include what has just happened; the past has no place in the discussion. Have this conversation in private.

"I noticed that you took a 35-minute coffee break. Do you know that the policy is only 15 minutes?" And then, as author Susan Scott says in her book *Fierce Conversations*, "Let silence do the heavy lifting.®" Do not say, "You always take long coffee breaks." This statement would begin an argument.

Sit back and wait. Expect an instant denial. Let the person vent and if it goes on too long, simply put your hand up, the universal sign for stop, and say, "I wanted to bring it to your attention because I don't think I have let you know that this is not acceptable, and I apologize. From now on, please check your watch when you leave, so you can come back in reasonable time. Can you imagine what would happen if everyone took long breaks?"

Keep A Record

After your conversation, take out a piece of paper, and jot down the date and a quick notation that outlines what you said and what your employee said. Start a file with your employee's name, and pop the paper in.

This is not the end. Consistency is the key. Note the breaks this employee takes in the next few days, and if they are within the time limit, thank him. If not, remind him again and write it down for his file.

This helps you decide if there is a pattern. Also, when it is time to do a written evaluation, you can make reference to actual incidents instead of something too general that may get you into a verbal tug-of-war over who said what. You have it recorded on paper.

No one is a mind reader. If you don't let people know when you are upset or when you are happy, or if you don't set out your expectations in a clear manner, you can't expect people to change.

Got It?

1. It's time to be honest and to assess a situation by looking at facts, not at what you feel or think. Record behavior that you think needs correcting to see if you are accurate.

2. Have I set expectations clearly with this employee, or have I simply assumed he or she "got it"?

3. Listen to your self-talk and notice extreme words. Consciously remove them from your vocabulary.

Chapter 3

Email Blues

When was the last time you sent a seemingly innocent email and someone phoned to apologize because they had upset you? Were you surprised? You shouldn't have been. Email is a form of communication that can elicit the strongest emotions, and those emotions are often anger or hurt.

Email is a great way to send information and an extremely poor way to communicate, or to build a relationship with another human being. In fact, when I made that statement at a recent provincial tourism conference, I received an outburst of spontaneous clapping, so it resounds with many. With email, no one can see your face, body language, or hear the cadence of your voice; therefore, it is easy to pick up the wrong message.

Face-To-Face

If you have something important to say, get up and walk to that person and have a face-to-face conversation. Or if that is impossible, pick up the phone. At least when you are on the phone you can listen carefully to verbal clues and you can use your voice tone to project your meaning.

I have had staff members complain that no one answered their emails. I would say, "Get up off your chair and go and talk to the person. Show them that you care and are interested enough to chat. You want people to remember you? Make personal contact." They were usually amazed at the great conversations they had when they did a face-to-face.

The Evils of "Reply All"

I remember one of my new staff members sharing a potentially CLM (career limiting move) when she was working at a busy communications agency. She had managed a project for a particularly difficult client, and when it was completed, she sent an email to her boss to say how relieved she was to have survived this woman's wrath. She went into details about the woman's foolish and often impossible requests and how grateful she was that her boss coached her through this difficult situation. Unfortunately, instead of hitting reply, she hit reply all and her message went directly to the client.

With a red face and heavy heart, she immediately phoned the client and apologized. The client listened and then said, "Thank you for letting me know. We all make mistakes when we first start in a career and while this won't be your last, I hope you will take the lesson from it. I realize I was difficult. I don't make excuses and I'm glad you don't either!"

The employee's next stop was her boss, and as she relayed the story, her boss listened intently and then said that she was lucky that this woman showed understanding because she was a million dollar client and one the boss was not ready to lose. Then he cautioned her that should there ever be a next time, the first step should be to check in with the boss. If the client had not understood, the boss needed to be ready for a call.

While this story turned out okay, many don't. Because email

is a quick way to touch base with others, we often do it in a hurry and that's when mistakes and misunderstandings happen.

Next time you go to send an email, ask yourself, "Is this information or communication?" If the answer is communication, make a phone call or go and see the person. The time spent will pay off later on.

Take Your Time

If you are angry and want to vent, by all means write the email and then send it . . . to yourself! Give it twenty-four hours, reread it, and then make a judgment with your more logical, cooler mind. Will this help or hurt? Is this something that in the big scheme of things will make a positive difference? Also consider that written words will form a permanent record that could be used against you at some point.

Email can be a boon or an obstruction. Don't hide behind your keyboard. Go out and build relationships with the people you care about. The time will be worth it.

Got It?

1. Is there a better way to communicate with this particular person or about this particular project than email?

2. Once you hit send, your words are there forever. Are they up to the scrutiny of posterity?

Chapter 4

Silence Opens Doors

For thirty years we have made a point of keeping in touch with a fellow who was once my husband's boss. Why? It's because this man is the very best listener we have ever met. No matter where we meet, he asks about our kids by name, our extended families, and for updates on significant issues we talked about last time we met. He is amazing. He makes us feel we are important to him.

Who really listens to you and who is merely waiting for their turn to talk? If you have one or two key people in your life who actually listen, you are indeed lucky. When you think about with whom you have long-term relationships and why, you will often come back to, "This person listens to me."

Good communication is all about building relationships, and a large part of the relationship is listening. The saying, "God gave you two ears and one mouth and you should use them accordingly," rings true. You glean so much information by sitting back and really hearing what someone else is saying. By listening and occasionally recapping, the speaker will share details and facts to help you understand.

Stop, Look, and Listen!

When others come to you with problems, listen. You will discover that they often have their own solutions. They were merely looking for a sounding board. As you summarize what they have told you, you will observe that they nod with a, "Yes, she gets it" look on their face.

If you can hardly wait to share your own experience or proffer advice, you will quickly shut them down, making them feel as though their stories are unimportant, their issues of no great consequence, and, worse still, that they don't matter. Have you ever been on the phone telling a story to a friend, only to hear a keyboard clacking away, or noticed a distracted tone in the listener's voice? How did you feel?

One of my friends said that when she overheard her former husband talk about her, it became evident that he had never listened to her and really didn't know her. It made her feel insignificant. Have you ever had that experience? A person who doesn't listen is not a person you want to build a relationship with.

A participant at a workshop I was giving in Vancouver said that she has a friend who shares lots of information. Her first question when the friend starts sharing is, "Do you want me to give advice, or do you simply want to share?" This helps her identify her role in the conversation. That's a good idea, especially when you already have a good relationship with the other person. Questions can be a large part of listening as long as they are for clarification. Do not try to direct the speaker on a path you think they need to take by asking leading questions.

Quick Fix

In some of my workshops, I ask participants to turn to a partner and for three minutes to share the details of their past week.

They are to practice listening skills and to nod and maintain eye contact. They are not to give advice, nor to tell their own stories. Then they switch and repeat the process.

Afterward, I ask how it felt to talk for three minutes. The most common answer is, "I ran out of things to say." This illustrates that we all have time to give our undivided attention to another, especially for three minutes. In our busy world, however, we often want to rush the person out of our door so we can get on with our day.

When asked, "What is one quality you value in a boss?" the top quality is, "He or she listens to me." Because the boss listens, the employee feels appreciated and respected. Employees will then work harder and create better products.

Author Henri J.M. Nouwen said, "When we honestly ask which persons in our lives mean the most to us, we often find that it is those who, instead of giving much advice, solutions, or cures, have chosen rather to share our pain and touch our wounds with a gentle tender hand."

Start to listen today. Listening is just as important, possibly more important, than talking.

Got It?

1. Who in your life needs to be heard? Next time you meet with them, you are only allowed to nod and recap what they have said. No advice, no reference to a past experience you've had. You'll find out that you have begun to build a lasting relationship.

2. Don't you have three minutes?

Chapter 5

Do One Thing Well

There are a number of studies saying that human brains are not made for multi-tasking. When we switch from one task to another, our performance often goes down. So multi-tasking can cost companies and organizations thousands of dollars.

On top of the financial cost, I believe that multi-tasking has an emotional cost, especially in communication. When we multi-task, we eliminate that feeling of self-satisfaction that comes when we complete a job.

When we multi-task, we feel we have never finished. We never get closure and we become anxious as we try to juggle too many balls at once. Most times, this leads to frustration and anxiety.

When we communicate, we need to give our total focus to the audience with whom we are having the conversation, whether it is in person, electronically, via phone, or on paper. When we multi-task, we become distracted, and our audience is quick to sense our lack of attention and will feel under-valued.

I once had a boss who had so many tasks to complete that she would often say, "I can do my email while we talk." Perhaps a few talented people can accomplish two things at once. Most of us cannot.

Communication Is A Two-Way Street

If you don't give your full attention to each conversation, what message are you sending to that audience? Are they not worthy of your time? Is what they are saying so insignificant that you have no need to listen? How does that build a trusting relationship?

I also believe that multi-tasking can happen internally as well as externally. Think about conversations you have when, as the other person was speaking, you found your mind going to your happy place or formulating a response or mentally writing a to-do list.

While you may know the speaker can't actually see what is going on, most times, she or he can sense your lack of focus. As you multi-task, your eyes become glazed and if you do answer, your voice pitch may be different. Often there is wariness in your response, a sure sign that you are not interested in what is being said.

Distract Yourself

When I teach communication courses for media spokespeople, a key point is to put them out of their comfort zone by asking them to stand up and turn their back to their desk when they are on the phone. That way, they have no distractions. Try it.

You want to be on your toes so you hear everything that is said. Then your responses are accurate and carry your message forward. Shouldn't you share that same courtesy with those with whom you work daily?

I once worked on a web design committee and our conversations were all over the map about the direction the design should take. Finally, the project manager held up his hand. We stopped talking, and he said, "This is a go for the next sparkly thing conversation. Let's focus."

What he was saying was that we never completed one thought or idea before someone else spoke and took us in another direction. If we were going to achieve anything, we had to settle on one thing and see it through to completion. Are you reaching for the next "sparkly" before you have completed the last one?

I challenge you to adopt the "one thing well" approach. At the beginning of each day, think about what conversations and communication pieces you will be working on, make a list, order them, and then begin. No! Don't reach for the "sparkly one." Complete the first task before reaching for the next.

Got It?

1. What must be accomplished before I go home? What is the non-negotiable?

2. What other goals do I have for today?

3. Am I asking too much of myself?

Chapter 6

Are You Giving Piano Lessons?
We've Got To Start Meeting Like This

My kids took piano lessons because I took piano lessons. Did I like piano lessons? No. Did my kids? No. Just because you did it, or your company always did it, it does not mean it's the correct thing to do.

Over and over, I see senseless meetings happening where hundreds of thousands of dollars are tied up in the human resources sitting at the table accomplishing absolutely nothing to create a better team or company. Why? Because the company has always done it this way. Couldn't meetings be done better?

There never needs to be a meeting to share information or factual items. Let your staff be responsible for reading that sort of information, and if they have questions or comments, they can ask the source directly.

Meetings, Meetings Everywhere, and No One Stopped To Think!

Start asking yourself, "Why do we have meetings?" Just because you've always had Monday morning meetings, or specific positions always attend a certain meeting does not mean it is the best way to accomplish the work at hand. Do a personal inventory of the meetings you attend. Which ones help move the company ahead? What types of agenda items do you need to move your team or company forward?

Decide who really needs to come to each meeting and be ruthless about which items need to be handled in a group setting and which ones can be handled differently. Some people want to go to all the meetings and their days are spent behind closed doors while their own team suffers from their lack of involvement. Truthfully evaluate who needs to be at what meeting. When you do cut back on numbers, define how others will be notified of decisions.

Come up with some group rules. Often information items such as dates and times, decisions already approved, and upcoming agenda items can be sent out via email. No one needs to read informational PowerPoint slides to the group.

Meetings should handle items that need conversations and involvement from a variety of people. Membership to meetings could change according to what is being discussed. Agenda items must be sent well in advance of the meeting so everyone comes with key points and ideas. Then conversation can be honest and robust.

Change It Up

Set time limits on each agenda item and stick to them. Make sure everyone is heard from and, if the discussion needs to go longer, set another day; or ask for consensus from the group to carry on; or table another item so this one can be completed.

Set a revolving chair for your meetings. This was one of the best things I ever did with my team. It allowed for growth of all members and I also saw some wonderful leadership qualities in members I had not seen before. It also made everyone feel more involved. Some team members were reluctant to take on the role; however, after some encouragement they enjoyed the experience.

After each meeting, write down the two or three key points you want every member to pass along to their team so everyone is getting the same message. Also make note of who will do what, so there is no miscommunication later on.

Then send this information out to all those with a need to know. Why keep it secret? That way, everyone is responsible for keeping themselves informed and finger-pointing will end. Meeting attendees can also share this information face-to-face with their team members.

When you keep everyone informed and use your meeting time wisely, open, honest communication will follow and people will come to the table with more constructive attitudes.

Got It?

1. Which meetings make you feel energized and valued? Which ones leave you wondering why?

2. Examine the next agenda. Are there spots where changes can be made?

3. Look at who comes to your meetings and calculate what each meeting costs. Are you getting value for this investment? For instance, if you have eight people attending and the average hourly rate for each is $150 and the meeting lasts two hours, you have just cost the company $2,400. Was this a good investment?

Chapter 7

Cut Yourself Off

By mastering these two words, "Got it," many communication woes will disappear. That's the advice Sam Horn, author and international public speaker, gave me at a recent training course.

"Too often people don't know when to stop a conversation," she said. "They keep asking for more feedback or more examples. What often happens is the person who wanted to help begins to 'cloud over' as he sees precious minutes or even hours slipping away. It's not the way to build a relationship."

Have you ever had a colleague or a friend ask for feedback or assistance with a project, then, when you begin to give it, they ask more and more questions or present more and more excuses or rationalizations about why your suggestions or comments won't work? You begin to wonder why they ever asked in the first place. And the next time that person asks for help, you might be reluctant to respond to them.

Three-Second Window

Studies show that it takes about three seconds for a person to get a first impression of you. If you want people to be willing to help you, guard their time carefully. If something they have said does need clarification, think about what one or two direct questions will help you understand and then ask them as briefly as possible. Stay away from any excuses or debate about their statements. Always thank them for their precious time and then leave.

If you know that sometimes you have a difficult time "putting a sock in it," practice. Rehearse what you will say before you make a request for feedback and then stick to those points. When they share helpful information with you, smile, look them in the eye, and say, "Got it."

Brevity is valued. Learn to be brief or you'll get grief.

Got It?

1. Before you ask for help or feedback, carefully craft your words so there is no possibility of being misunderstood. Think about what specific question you are asking. Write your questions, be specific, and practice asking them out loud before you seek help.

2. At meetings, if asked for opinions, give one or two brief points, and then stop talking.

Chapter 8

Key Messages

I once had a college professor as my coaching client. She was overly concerned and anxious about staff meetings because she became tongue-tied when it was time to say something. It was such a problem that she said she preferred a root canal to a staff meeting.

She said she became a babbling fool when she presented her thoughts, coming across as totally incompetent and negative. She felt that she often lost out on opportunities for her department because she tended to be incoherent. As a result, she feared that team members trivialized her and did not understand her role.

We are our own worst critics and I'm quite sure this wasn't always the impression she gave. In order to help her turn the situation around, I asked her to name two things about her faculty role that she would like everyone at that leadership table to remember about her.

We brainstormed for a while and came up with three, as well as illustrations to each point. Her key points were:

1. She was experienced in teaching a variety of subjects, from children's literature to language arts and writing.

2. She enjoyed the challenge of developing new courses.

3. She had over twenty years experience teaching college-level courses in the Aboriginal community as well as traditional college students.

It's Not Just What You Say

We talked about the importance of body language and came up with two techniques to bolster her image. She was to consciously check her posture, to sit up straight, and to look directly in the eye of a colleague as she spoke. When she arrived at the meeting, she was to spread out her materials and take up her space on the table as well as to look around and chat with others before the proceedings began. She was essentially staking out her territory.

Another technique she incorporated was to look for meaningful ways to contribute to meetings. She was to prepare before each meeting by looking at the agenda and jotting down a couple of points about one or two items she felt passionately about or had expertise in. This would enable her to anticipate questions and formulate replies so that she could comment or answer with confidence. Most of her answers and comments wove in at least one of her key messages. I said, "Look on it as a challenge. You are bright and articulate. Use those skills to make sure others come to realize it too."

We spent lots of time in practice sessions with her using her three key messages with short examples so that they flowed off her tongue. While she is a gifted communicator in the classroom, she needed to work on projecting that confidence at meetings.

Be Your Own Cheerleader

We also made sure that she would not apologize or put herself down. She would speak positively when she commented, keep the points brief, and back them up with concrete examples of what worked, or if it hadn't, the lesson that had been learned.

Then we talked about how to bridge back to those messages when someone was trying to take her off track. Media spokespeople for companies soon learn that you don't have to directly answer the media's questions; instead, you can bridge back to what you want the public to hear. She could do the same. Looking very confident and eager to answer, you use phrases like, "The real issue here is . . ." or, "What you may not know is . . ." or, "That is not true," and then use a bridging statement to loop back to one of your key messages.

Never repeat any negative comments because you have just imprinted those words onto the listener's mind for a second time, and if they hear it a third time, it sticks! When you work in communications, you know that, in order to impart any message, a listener must hear it at least three times. Therefore, you want to ensure it is your message they hear.

Give Yourself The Gift Of Time

If someone asks you a question or seeks your opinion and you are really stuck, you can say, "I want to take some time to think about that and will be in touch later today or first thing tomorrow." You are projecting that you want to give the best answer and are not someone who speaks without thinking. Be sure to follow-up.

If they say they can't wait and it is a yes/no type question then say, "If I need to give an answer now, it is no; if you can wait until I have time to think about it, I will contact you with an answer that I hope will serve us all better. It still may not be the answer you want to hear; I would just like time to give it my best thinking."

My academic coaching client called me after her first meeting and said that people listened to her and she was able to get approval for one project that previously had been blocked. Over the next months, she saw a shift in her stature in the eyes of her leadership team. Occasionally they asked her opinion and, much to her delight, started to repeat some of her key messages.

She still struggles with feelings of inadequacy and trepidation before meetings. I agree that, while it may never be easy, she now has some tools to help her project her real self. With thoughtful planning and preparation, we can all be heard.

Got It?

1. What are three qualities you want every colleague to know about you?

2. Think up one simple example that illustrates each quality.

3. Have you looked over the agenda and thought about possible comments or questions that colleagues may ask before each meeting? Jot down your thoughts.

4. Practice, out loud, weaving your key messages into everyday conversations.

Chapter 9

Nip It In The "But"

Most people are shocked by how many times they use the word *but* in a day. I challenge you to put an elastic band on your wrist and each time you hear yourself say *but,* give it a snap. Many of us will have red wrists at the end of the day. By the way, the word *however* is exactly the same!

"I like the way you managed that event but next time, can you make sure I approve the program?" While you might think you are giving a compliment, what did the receiver actually hear? "There must have been something wrong with the program." What will they remember? That they messed up because they should have let you see the program. While you thought you were giving help- ful feedback, the receiver of the message felt deflated and hurt. Any phrase that follows the word *but* holds a much stronger place in the listener's memory than whatever preceded the *but*.

Remember getting your report card? If your parents were reading it aloud and they read, "She is doing well in math, but she should practice her times tables more," didn't your stomach drop the minute you heard *but*? You knew you'd be getting drilled on the times tables every night. I can't repeat too many times: any phrase that follows the word *but* erases anything said before it.

Show Stopper

Want to stop a conversation? Use the word *but*. "That's a good idea but we've tried it before." Right away the receiver of the message has had the verbal door slammed. It sounds as though there is no way you are going to listen to anything else she says on that topic. Instead, if you said, "That's a good idea and I've heard it before," it sounds a lot more open-minded and as if you are ready to listen.

Without meaning to, the minute you use *but* in a sentence, people often stop listening to you. They begin to form a rebuttal in their heads. While forming this rebuttal, they will not hear anything else you say.

For instance, try having a debate with another person about whether or not it is best to be single or married. During your discussion, you are not allowed to use the word *but*. You will be amazed to discover that you have a discussion, not an argument and neither voices nor tempers rise.

When you use the word *but* right away, it feels like you are putting blame on someone or showing them why they are wrong. When you use the word *and*, it comes across as two statements with no judgment or blame. You will build positive relationships with others if you get rid of the word *but*.

Every time you go to say *but*, substitute the word *and*. You will soon find that people are much more agreeable. You will think you are not making sense or that you sound odd, or that using *and* is grammatically awkward. People don't hear that; instead, they hear someone who is agreeable and values their input.

If at first, you find it difficult to substitute *and*, stop and take a breath, and begin a new sentence. You are essentially putting in a period. Again, you may think you are being too slow and people will want your words to speed up. Not true; what people will hear is someone who is willing to hear their ideas.

Now you have begun to lose *but* in spoken communication, there are two other places to rid yourself of the pesky little word. First, take all the *buts* out of any written communication. This will take a little mental elbow grease and cause you to rework sentences. It will be worth the effort.

Be Kind

Second, and possibly more important, is to take *but* out of your self-talk. How you speak to yourself will dictate how you speak to others. If you are not kind to yourself, how can you be kind or expect others to be kind to you? No more beating yourself up with statements like, "That was good, but if I'd taken more time it would have been better," or "I like the way it turned out, but Sally could have done it better." Stop the mean self-talk! You did the best you could and now you can look to the future.

Get rid of that big, ugly *but* today!

Got It?

1. Listen to yourself for the next twenty-one days. How often do you use the word *but*? Stop it!

2. Once you have written a report, memo, evaluation, or news-letter, use the search mode of your computer program to seek out all the *buts*. Rework the sentence so there are no *buts* or *howevers*.

3. Observe at meetings and interactions with people, listening for the word *but*. Watch body language and the words that fol-low after a *but* is spoken.

Chapter 10

Back To The Future

If we beat ourselves up about what could have or should have happened, we will never move forward. Too often, we are so busy regretting what happened, or didn't happen, that we forget to focus on where we want to go.

Many communication experts tell us that if you remove two simple words from your vocabulary, your life will change. The words? *Should have*. What image does that phrase conjure up? Someone shaking their finger at you and telling you to change the past? Who can change the past? As soon as you hear it, you feel hopeless and helpless.

When I was nineteen, I worked summers at a city golf course. My boss communicated by yelling and making accusations. He was a bully and most of us dreaded his visits because his behavior was full of *could haves* and *should haves* sprinkled with sputtering, finger shaking, flashing eyes, and a red face.

I worked with a very meek, petite woman who had been there years and was the target of most of his tirades. He came bursting in one day and exploded, "Darla, don't you know that you dump the garbage from one bag into another? I see three bags half full. What a waste!" And with that he threw the bags at the quaking Darla.

'Fess Up

I was taught to own up to my mistakes and the sooner the better, so before Darla replied, I stepped forward and said, "That was my fault. I did it and Darla didn't know. From now on, I will only use one bag." He stood there open- mouthed and then said, "Darla should have told you!" Poor Darla; even when I admitted it was my mistake, she was still blamed.

That was not fair, so I looked at him and said, "Mr. Jones, Darla did not know I was emptying the bags. We cannot change the past. I can change the future."

Darla was trying to blend into the woodwork because I had "talked back" to the red-faced, sputtering Mr. Jones. He abruptly turned on his heel and high-tailed it out of the clubhouse to attack some other poor staff member.

Never again did Mr. Jones attack Darla when I was around. He would come sputtering in and then say, "Girls, did you know that . . ." Or, "From now on could you . . ."

Model Behavior

I was also taught it is important to teach people how you want to be treated and what behavior you will and will not tolerate. You model back what you expect. No yelling, no meanness, no emotion; just simple statements uttered in a direct, quiet, calm manner.

When you point at someone and then deliver, *should haves* you take away all hope that the person can change that experience. He or she is powerless because it happened in the past. Also, you are giving the recipient of the message the perfect opportunity to think, "I can't change it, so what a jerk you are for bringing it up."

When you use words like *from now on* or *next time*, the responsibility shifts to the future, where changes can be made. It will be up to the person to perform correctly next time. You become the coach, not the critic, and you show that you value them and their ability to moderate their behavior.

If you are two or 102, you always know what you *should have* done. If someone values you enough to bring an issue to your attention and then trusts you to work together to solve it, your respect for that person grows. The relationship grows and communication improves.

Good communication is all about building honest, trusting relationships. Begin today by removing *should have* from your vocabulary.

Got It?

1. Listen to your self-talk as well as the way you speak to others. Eliminate *should haves* and *could haves*. Substitute *from now on* or *next time*.

2. Think back to a time when you said *should have* to someone and come up with better responses.

3. As you watch others, listen for a *should have* and then observe how the receiver acts.

Chapter 11

Lower The Bar

Too often we set our personal expectations so high that not even Superwoman or Superman could meet our goals. Whether it is for our relationships with others, or the work we do, it's time to consider just what we are asking of ourselves.

- Is it realistic?
- Will it matter in five days, five months, or five years if "it" is not quite perfect?

These two simple questions will give you a gauge to assist you to set realistic personal goals that are specific, attainable, measurable, and have a time limit.

If a report is due in three days, you might say to yourself, "I will devote six hours to pulling together this report. I will notify Jennifer and Brendan that I will have the report to them by three p.m. tomorrow to check the numbers, and they will need to have it back to me by ten a.m. the following day."

When you give yourself a time limit, you are much more likely to complete the work in that time. Once you have assembled the important information, had the numbers checked, and are sure that the report answers the questions it was supposed to, put it away and begin your next task. Good enough is usually good enough. Not everything has to be a work of art.

Look at what needs to be completed. Make a list of each project; write down the time you expect it to take and who needs to approve or contribute, and then block that time into your day. If you find out you have set unachievable goals, prioritize and let your boss know.

Tough Questions

There is a saying, "If you want a job done, ask busy people." If you always work late, come in on most weekends, and never complain to your boss, he or she thinks you are enjoying it. Your boss can't be a mind reader. It's time to engage in an honest conversation with yourself, and then with your boss.

Ask yourself questions like, "Why do I think I have to do it all?" and "Is there a better or different way to accomplish this?"

Make a list of what has to be achieved and the time you expect it to take, and then ask your boss which priority you should begin with, or for ideas on how you can handle the multiple tasks together. Before you meet, prepare some suggestions for how everything can be accomplished without you doing it all.

You might get a gruff, "I want everything done," or "Hire someone else to help." Anticipate these types of reactions before you go in and be ready to calmly answer, "I wish I could; now which one is most important?" Or, "If I had more time to train a new person, that would be a great idea. I'll keep it in mind for next time. Now, which one is your priority?" Or, "I know these are all important; let's brainstorm and try to come up with some workable solutions. I know that Jim, in accounting, has some expertise in this area, or Susan, in public affairs, has expressed interest in working in my department."

Silence Is Golden

As author Susan Scott says in her book *Fierce Conversations*, "Let silence do the heavy lifting."® Succinctly say what you need to say and then throw the verbal ball back in their court. Your eyes can toss it back. You do not need to fill the empty space with chat; it is as much their issue to solve as yours. Remain non-confrontational, calm, and remember you are there to share information and to come up with solutions that work for everyone.

You'll be surprised that once you set boundaries with your time, both internally and externally, others will step up and help; sometimes you'll discover that what was a rush can, all of a sudden, be moved or delayed.

Be Still and Plan

Allow thinking time each day, to breathe deeply and then consider, "What is really important here?" and "Will it matter tomorrow?" Lowering the bar for yourself gives you permission to do the best job you can with the time you have. No guilt allowed.

If you have jumped onto the express lane of life and it is speeding faster and faster, like a never-ending auger, and you feel as though you are about to drop off the end into nothingness, it's time to slam the "slow down" lever, close your eyes, and prioritize. Not everything has to be done immediately and perfectly. And you do not need to do it all!

Consider for a moment what would happen if you dropped dead. Would that important work still get done? You know what? It would. Do you have to do it all and in no time at all? Does it have to be perfect? Only you can make that choice.

One of my favorite sayings is, "Anyone who 'does it all' should be quarantined." When you try to "be it all" professionally and personally, you are always going to feel disappointment. Give yourself permission to be good enough. It is not often we actually have to be perfect. Know the few times you do.

Got It?

1. Block off at least ten minutes first thing in the morning, after lunch, and before you end your day to stop, be totally still, and think. Be strict with yourself and guard this time. Weigh the pros and cons of the goals you set, lower the bar when you can, and then say, "I'm doing the best I can with the time I have."

2. If someone is pushing your buttons and asking you to do more and more, it's time to have an honest conversation. Write down two or three (no more) points you wish to make. Practice the conversation at home in front of a mirror. Think through possible reactions and plan thoughtful responses to them. Then book an appointment. It's time to start a conversation; and remember, keep it brief or they will give you grief.

3. Are you expecting too much from yourself? You can't be everything to everyone. Make time each day to have honest conversations with yourself. Be as kind to yourself as you are to your best friend.

Chapter 12

Anti-Jekyll And Hyde

During a presentation to the banking industry, a member of the audience asked, "How do I talk with a staff member who is so up and down I never know what person I will be working with on a particular day?" Another person immediately spoke up and said, "Hey, my boss is the same way. One day he is charming and the next he is nasty."

You can't delay confronting undesirable behavior, because if you don't, people will think it's acceptable and the behavior may even escalate.

"Have you pointed out this behavior in one-on-one discussions?" I asked. The answer was, "Sort of." "Sort of" doesn't work. Unless you say it in black and white, the majority of these bullies will take from the conversation exactly what they wish, and most likely not what you mean.

Don't Sweep It Under The Rug

When you have someone who is "nice Joan" one day and "grumpy Joan" the next, let Joan know how she is acting. The minute you see behavior that has to change, call Joan into a private meeting. Look her in the eye and calmly and seriously say, "I noticed this morning when the receptionist handed you a message, you grabbed it and walked off. What is going on? Can you imagine how you made our receptionist feel?"

Any time you confront bad behavior, no matter what the age of the person, most likely she will deny it or make excuses. "I was in a hurry. Other things were on my mind. I have so much to do."

Look very serious and say something like, "I value all my employees and expect everyone to be treated with respect. When you rushed by with not even a good morning or a thank you, you sent a message that she was not important. I hope that is not true."

If it is your boss, you might say something along the lines of, "Gosh, yesterday you gave me accolades for the way my staff completed that project and today you are telling me that it was not up to your expectations. What is going on?"

Leave out how their actions make you feel because they will use that against you. If you say, "I feel upset when . . .", their most likely response will be, "Get thicker skin." Instead, use the word *you*. "You need to treat me with respect."

End the meeting by standing up, smiling, and saying something like, "I just want to let you know what I see. I hope it helped."

Don't use phrases like "I think you" because you have no idea what that person is thinking; just state the facts. Feedback statements do not have to take long. The shorter the message, the more impact it will have. You are simply helping the other person understand what you think.

Record And File It

After each meeting, make a quick note of what was said and date it. Put it into a file folder with the employee or your boss's name on it. A couple of lines are all that is needed. "I said," and "she said." This will help you decide if there is a pattern. The notes will reference real incidents and will be of assistance when you write up performance evaluations.

Recording what was said helps you keep things in perspective, especially if you are in work overload. Sometimes, you begin to think "she always" or "he never" and when you look in the file, you will see that the behavior happened a month ago, so it isn't a pattern. Writing down who said what and when, will keep things in perspective and will help you make a decision on how to proceed.

For some people, drawing inappropriate behavior to their attention is enough to stop the behavior; others may need a reminder. If after several reminders, the behavior persists, and it is something you can't live with, you may decide that it is best to make this person available to the industry. If it is your boss, you may decide to seek employment elsewhere.

Conversely, as the leader, you must witness when the employee does it right. Again, bring her in for a private meeting and point out the positive behaviors. You want your employees to know you notice the good things they do, too.

There may be some employees who never need corrective feedback. Even so, hold short, private meetings with them after something went well, because they are watching and, if you are spending all your time with the difficult ones, they may feel they aren't living up to your expectations.

Respectful, honest feedback, focusing only on facts is a critical first step to building trusting relationships.

Got It?

1. Are you ignoring bad or good behavior? What do you need to say to an employee today?

2. After any one-on-one, together summarize what has been said, so you know the message you wanted to send is the one received. A simple, "So let's summarize what we've discussed in two key points," will give you a gauge as to whether or not you were clear in your communication.

Chapter 13

Drain, Drain, Go Away

Is there someone in your life who, when you see them coming, you have a serious desire to become lonesome? Does this person drain you, and do you feel worse after the visit? It's time to take a test.

Answer these five questions to help you decide whether you will take some time to build the relationship into one of more mutual sharing, or whether it is time to cut your losses and move on to people who build you up rather than drag you down.

When talking to this person:

1. Does he ever ask you to share your thoughts or feelings?

2. Do you spend most of your time trying to cheer this person up?

3. Does this person get you thinking that there are some rough patches in your life that you weren't aware of before?

4. Does your stomach drop when you see his number on call display or the whites of his eyes?

5. Would your life be happier without this person?

Be A Steward Of Your Own Well-Being

If you answered yes to at least two of these questions, it's time to assess where the relationship is going and then to decide if the time invested is worth it; not to be hard-hearted, simply to be a steward of your own well-being. While we all have needy times, some people become continuous drains, and if we don't reduce or eliminate our time with them, we begin to display some of their traits.

Draw A Line In The Sand

If this person is a colleague, it's time to set some boundaries. When he arrives, hold your hand up in the universal "stop" signal and say, "Is this important or can it wait until I've finished this?" If he insists it's important, give him five minutes and then use the hand signal again and say, "I wish I had time to listen longer; I don't. We can rebook when I am finished with this project." Or, "I wish I had longer; let's rebook after work, or go for breakfast tomorrow morning." Immediately break eye-contact and get back to work. I find that these time-wasters usually are only interested in chatting during company time and not so keen on using their own free time, so the second statement often works well.

I once had a boss who loved to come into my office and tell me long stories. The time I sat and listened was usually made up by me in the evening when he was home enjoying his family. One day I decided that my time was important, too, and I was willing to take a risk and see if I could change his behavior.

As soon as he would arrive, I'd subtly check my watch and give him five minutes. Once the five minutes was up, I said,

"Wow, we've spent five minutes on this and now I have to get back to work if you want some good things from me today."

The first time, he just smiled and kept going, so I waited another five and said, "Alright then," summarized his information, and then stood up and said, "Excuse me, I have to go to the washroom." He looked shocked, and when I returned, he was gone.

This happened about four times, and I think he thought I must have had some condition; however, the next time I looked at my watch and said, "I've got to get back to work," he left. Of course I exercised my judgment. If the conversation was about work, or an issue that we needed to deal with, then time was spent. I was always polite and smiled as I dismissed him.

The Brighter Side

If this drain is always negative, you might want to encourage the person to change their behavior. One of the first questions to ask when she begins her lament is, "So what went well today?" Or, "Tell me one positive thing you learned from that experience." This gets the person to stop and begin to reprogram or reframe their conversation.

If you have a long-term relationship with the person, you can try a little humor with a non-verbal "playing of a violin," or a quip such as, "You are a dreary one today." Or, "Hi, happy!" Or, after you have listened to a long sad story, shake your eye brows and say, "That went so well for you; now let's talk about me!" and laugh. Sometimes the shock value gives them the jolt they need in order to really begin to hear what they are saying.

It may take an honest heart-to-heart to refocus someone who has gotten into the "poor me" position. Try phrases like, "Every time we talk, you are so negative that I feel worse than when we started. In the past, I've given you suggestions or advice and it doesn't seem to help. I feel sorry that you are so unhappy and I also feel that always talking about it does not help you or me. From now on, when you begin, I will give you three or five minutes to be negative and vent. Then I am going to stop you, and you will give me three or five minutes to talk. After that, we can only share good things."

If you are like many people, and have more friends, relatives, and acquaintances than you have time for, it's always good to ask: "Is this a relationship worth working at or am I always giving and never getting a thing back, except maybe a headache or a heavy heart?" If the answer is, "I'm expending more than I'm getting," it's time to say, "Drain, drain go away!" and begin to withdraw.

Give yourself permission to clean house and become responsible for the people you invite in. Remember that you don't need to be a friend to everyone. Set some boundaries. You will feel better and the chances are, the other person will take your advice and be glad you were honest; or if he is content to be negative, he will move to the next person who will lend him a listening ear.

We are all the boss of ourselves. We can choose to be a doormat and listen until our hearts are sore and work late each evening, or we can choose to give our precious time to people who buoy us up. You are not being nasty when you choose where to spend your time; you are being kind to yourself.

Got It?

1. Who in your work life is robbing you of your time? What can you do about it? Make a plan.

2. Which friends make you feel better after seeing and talking to them? Are you spending enough time with them?

Chapter 14

Authentic People

Have you ever met someone who on the outside appears kind and caring and yet after talking with this person, you often feel off-balance and insecure? It all comes down to whether or not the person is authentic. To me, being authentic means being sincere. Conversely, inauthentic people subtly and cunningly change their words and actions just like a chameleon changes its colors.

A friend and I were discussing why we like some people and others not so much. It usually comes down to whether or not they are authentic in their non-verbal and verbal communication. Young children are great for picking out those who are sincere. Think about to whom children gravitate; they are usually kind, caring and, I would say, authentic people.

Inauthentic people give mixed messages and then blame you for misinterpreting what was said. They twist your words so they become the victims and you the perpetrator, or the message they give to others in no way resembles what you actually said. Inauthentic people enjoy a good sulk when their under-handed techniques do not work and they may even lie about what was said if it makes them look good.

As adults, we have to interact with all manner of people. Sometimes our ability to recognize inauthentic people becomes clouded, or we ignore important indicators, especially if this behavior has been going on for some time. We often think it is us and so we try harder to understand, blaming ourselves for our inability to understand this person, or we wonder what we are doing wrong. Stop it! It's not you!

Inauthentic people have been acting like this for years. They do lots of talking, and their follow-through is negligible. You often feel as though you cannot depend on an inauthentic person because you can't trust what they will do with the conversation you have had. Therefore, you are guarded with the information you share.

They often use phrases like, "Oh, you misunderstood me," or "I was just trying to be helpful," or "You should have been more specific."

Why Didn't That Feel Good?

Because some people have been allowed to be inauthentic for so long it has become a habit. For instance, they may give you a compliment but it doesn't give you a boost. "Oh, you are just like me, so good at juggling many balls." "Joan said you are so organized, just like me."

They will inquire how you are doing and, before you have time to answer, they go into a long monologue about themselves. Or, it feels as though they are asking you questions about a difficult situation, not to ascertain how you feel nor to see if there is a way to help, but to make themselves feel better. "How many people attended that event you hosted? Oh, just twenty? Hmm… interesting. I wonder where everyone was."

Another tactic inauthentic people use is the ambush method. They hit you with hurtful words and leave. "I really wish I could go but you already made the plans." They imply you didn't want them. Before you can respond, they are gone and you are feeling cruel. When you stop and think about what just happened, you realize they never meant to come; they just want you to feel guilty.

If a relative or a long-term friend is inauthentic, you might want to try some corrective approaches. First, set boundaries and be consistent and clear as to what is acceptable to you.

Don't Lie Down And Take It!

Choose one specific behavior to change and then have a private conversation. The inauthentic person does not lose face and you can state consequences. Stay unemotional and stay on-message. (Refer to Chapter Eight)

Second, don't let them pull you down rabbit holes. They will twist your words so you get side-tracked or, all of a sudden, they'll say, "You are so sensitive." Don't take the bait. Calmly restate your message.

Keep A Hard Copy

If you work with an inauthentic colleague or staff member, make sure that instructions are written down, agreements initialed, and when possible, have conversations in front of witnesses, as the inauthentic person is less likely to deny incidents if someone can refute their version of events. After a conversation, send a quick email outlining what you decided, deadlines, and who is responsible for each piece.

Inauthentic people are often quick to compliment someone and then as soon as they are out of range, tell a different story. If they are critical to you about someone else, rather than hold your tongue so you appear to agree, speak up. Your response can be something like, "That's not been my experience." Or, "Why would you say that?"

If you know your words will be twisted in the retelling, say nothing and limit the amount of time you spend with this person.

If the inauthentic person is your boss, remember that there are some battles you just won't win. This type of boss is toxic to you and your organization, and morale suffers. Trying harder, working longer, and turning another cheek does not work.

Constant subtle, hurtful innuendoes will erode your confidence and your resilience. You will begin to doubt your abilities. My advice? Cut your losses and leave. Your physical and mental health is worth it.

No matter your role – employee, employer, parent, friend or colleague – the way you communicate and your authenticity will denote how you will get along with others. To build trust and relationships with others, you must strive to be authentic.

Got It?

1. Are you authentic in your communication? Listen to yourself for the next week.

2. Who makes you exhausted? Write down why.

3. Now decide if you are willing to overlook some of the qualities or if they are ones that you cannot ignore.

4. Write down a plan for your next steps.

Chapter 15

Trust Your Gut

If your gut says no – no means no! That's my mantra. Many times I've had a niggling feeling about something I'm about to do and I have ignored it. Later, I find out that had I listened, life would have been a lot less complicated.

Once, when I was desperate for help, I hired a person although alarm bells were ringing in my head, warning me not to believe her references. At the time, I thought it more important to hire a body than to trust my instincts.

Over the next year, this person, who had a pleasant personality and was a genuinely nice person, caused me more work than having nobody in her chair. I was continually picking up dropped balls and repairing the damage done to my team by one member not carrying her part of the load.

Ultimately, after countless sleepless nights and extreme angst, I had to make the person "available to the industry," all because I ignored the voice that was saying, "Joan, there is something not quite right here."

Can You Live With It?

One of the most difficult things to do both as a freelance writer and the manager of various teams is to push the send button, or to sign off for final approval. Whether it is a speech for the CEO or a newspaper article, when you hit send, you know your words will soon be on public display. And, once on display, everyone becomes a critic. (Like some of you right now because I started the last sentence with *and*!)

Every time I have thought, "I should just recheck that source or that fact," and then decided not to because "I have already done it," or because I have to credit my staff with being professional and doing the proper checks, it's come back to haunt me!

What would have taken perhaps thirty minutes has cost me or the company hours trying to correct the situation, or it has damaged a relationship that I had been building for many months or even years. Once, it meant shredding 100,000 newspapers; another time, it meant apologizing for the word *not* in a quote from an expert, which, in effect, made her give an inaccurate statement to a large audience.

Both times a little voice was saying, "Check it, Joan," and in my haste, I ignored it. Had I trusted my gut, I would have stopped and done that final scrutiny. There is a fine line to tread, because if you become a checker of everything, you will waste countless hours checking and re-checking things that really don't matter. It is up to you to pick the times when the stakes are high enough to say another check is warranted.

Give Them Some Credit

If you continually check and re-check the work of you staff, you will give them the message that they are not capable of anything. It is not the way to develop their confidence nor to build responsibility. You will soon have a team that doesn't bother because they know your obsessive habits.

If you are checking for accuracy, that's understandable. If you are checking because they are doing it differently from you, ask yourself if the end product is still okay. If it is, step away. Being able to delegate and not expecting everyone to do things the same way is an essential skill of leadership.

You have to have confidence in your staff or you will be in a state of inertia, but if that little voice is saying, "This doesn't feel quite right," trust it! You won't be sorry.

Got It?

1. Do you step back for a breather when you need to make an important decision? If not, how can you make time?

2. Ask yourself what impact will this have if I do not check it? If you can live with it, let it go. If it could have a ripple effect, check it!

Chapter 16

Do It Now: Nike Is Right!

No matter your job, a good part of your day is probably spent thinking about what you should be doing. Words like, "I'll file this later," or "I should be doing that" keep you moving from one sparkly object to the next, never completing one thing. What a waste of time.

Back in the 1980s, one of my colleagues gave me a sign that said, "Do it now!" She told me to put it above my desk so when I looked up, I could see it. Those three words made a huge difference in my life.

In those days, when I opened my mail, my first thought was, "I'll deal with that later." Instead, I would look at "the sign" and make a decision: file it, read it, throw it out. I would say to myself, "I should phone that expert to set up an interview time," and then look at the sign and pick up the phone. I became much more efficient.

I've had colleagues tell me that when they give me something to do, it gets done. I think the secret is that little sign. It commands me to deal with an item right now so I can free up my mind for the next task.

What if you can't deal with it immediately? Write it on a list, so that you are not cluttering your mind with trivial things and you can concentrate on the task at hand. Then once you have completed the task, check it off. Nothing feels better than being able to mark something off your list.

Three Magic Words

One of my executive assistants said that she had difficulty with time management. Like all executive assistants, she had countless interruptions during the day. People needing things "yesterday," or answering the phone, therefore, she found it difficult to complete her work. Over the years, she had attended various time management courses and incorporated some of the techniques into her routine and, yet, she was still struggling.

We were having a conversation for her yearly evaluation and I told her about the "Do it now" sign and how it had helped me. She smiled and said it sounded like something she'd like to try. The next time I was at her desk, there, on a recipe-size card in black, bold letters was Do It Now!

The transformation was remarkable. All of a sudden, things were not being forgotten, lists were created, and tasks were completed on time. She was delighted. She felt a sense of self-satisfaction because she was completing things and not starting one until the other was done. She felt hopeful instead of hopeless.

Volley Back With A Toss Of Your Eyes

We also discussed how to handle the multiple requests she handled. I gave her permission to toss the responsibility ball back to the person putting in the request (me included) and to say, "I have this and this to complete by day's end and now your request. All are important. Which do you want me to do first?" All of a sudden, the person who was making the request had to consider the other tasks in the queue and prioritize. This technique works well no matter what position you hold.

If the person was a bully and said, "All," or "That's your problem," her answer was, "I wish I was super human and could; the reality is I can't, so which do you want me to do first?" The key here was to clamp her mouth firmly shut, look the person in the eye, and let them make the decision.

It worked. Her question made the other person consider my assistant's workload and take responsibility for the decision. What was more important, the report she was preparing for the board meeting later that day or faxing a letter to a client? Over time, some of the people who were constantly giving her "quick jobs" (which we know never are), decided it was more efficient to handle it themselves. Or the job wasn't such a rush and it actually could be completed later that day.

My assistant's self-confidence grew because she was standing tall and controlling what she could control by shifting the responsibly back to where it belonged. She also began completing many more tasks each day rather than starting many and finishing few.

She no longer was a victim. Two quick communication strategies changed her life.

First she made a Do It Now! sign and put it up where she could see it. Second, she put the responsibility for the choice of tasks back with those who had the power to make the decision.

Can you do the same?

A postscript to this story: My assistant said that she got so tired of her "Do It Now" sign harping on her that one day she put up a sign saying "Already Done It! ☺"

Got It?

1. Make a sign that says "Do It Now!" and post it where you will see it.

2. Practice saying out loud, "I have this and this to do; which do you want me to do first?" Then clamp your mouth shut and throw the verbal ball back to the other person.

Chapter 17

Dissonant Values And Workplace Stress

Is the culture at your company more focused on getting to the top than doing the right thing? If it is, and you don't share the same values, you may be feeling off-balance. Some members within families don't share the same values and may feel askew and wonder why.

One of the first steps to take if you feel a disconnect is to assess your personal values. Most of us have not taken the time to do this. Write them down and then rank them.

Values might include: accountability, accuracy, open communication, thoughtful change, fairness, intensity, integrity, power, privacy, status, trust, independence, collaboration, team work, independence, creativity, honesty, reliability, tradition, etc.

Feelings of disconnect include: worry, unease, fatigue, or feeling incompetent. Most times these feelings are not your fault; it is because there is no synchronization between your values and those of your superiors.

I once took a contract communications position and my role was to improve internal and external communications. One of the first meetings I attended with my boss gave me a good idea of why he was having difficulty.

He began to talk and talk and talk. As a new employee, I was surprised that no one asked any questions or made any comments. Most people had their heads down.

One agenda item was presented by another colleague and a few people made a comment and one brave soul asked a question. The boss answered the question before the presenter had the opportunity. Needless to say, we went through the agenda in record time.

At the conclusion of the meeting, he said, "Any questions?" No one muttered a thing. We all got up and walked out.

Once back in his office, he looked at me and said, "Wasn't that a great meeting?" I was speechless. It was my first day on the job and I was quite sure this wasn't a great meeting.

Do The Right Thing

Since I had been hired to improve communications, I took a deep breath and said, "You know, when you asked how it was going, a few people seemed to be saying that some things were of concern. I heard one fellow say he was confused about job responsibilities for the new initiative and another said his staff was upset about the new parking policy. I was wondering why you didn't ask them to tell you more."

"Now, Joan," he retorted, "we are all grown-ups and there are going to be whiners and those who see the glass half-empty no matter where you work. I find it best to ignore them and get on with the agenda items."

I was speechless. It has been my experience that if someone asks a question or expresses a concern, they are hoping for a discussion or answers. Apparently this fellow operated on a different set of values.

Over the next few weeks, I became more and more disillusioned and distressed with the way my new boss communicated with the other employees. He never listened to anything anyone said and was only happy when he was lecturing or criticizing others. He kept lots of secrets, or gave information which could have helped many employees to a select few.

When I talked about the value of open, honest communication and the pitfalls of withholding valuable information, his comments were telling me that it was a waste of time to listen to people in lesser roles than his. When I did question him, he acted like I was betraying him, and began to withhold information I needed to do a good job.

Short-Term Pain For Long-Term Gain

For me, communications is all about building relationships, and it was becoming more and more clear that it wasn't going to happen at this spot. Although my bank account would suffer, I began to look for a new job. It was clear our values did not align.

Actions Speak Louder Than Words

While some companies carefully write up values statements and hang them in visible places, the truth only emerges in the way those values are enacted each day. Many places display inspirational value statements, many do not live them.

So if you are feeling a disconnect at work, or are feeling burned out, it is often because there is a misalignment of values. When your values align with those of the company, you will feel energized and happy to come to work each day.

It isn't your fault. Trying harder, working longer, and ignoring more won't help if your gut is telling you, "This isn't right."

Got It?

1. What are your values? Make a list. Prioritize and then choose the top five.

2. Do you live those values at work? If not, it might be time to look for something different.

3. Do you live those values at home? Think about your non-verbal actions as much as your words.

Chapter 18

Any Void In Information Leads To Miscommunication

Any time someone begins to tell me something and then leans in close and says, "But you can't tell anyone else," I become annoyed.

Granted, there are exceptions. If it is a human resources issue within a company, it must be kept private, just as some personal things are better left unsaid. Ultimately, you will have to be the judge.

What I'm talking about is information that others will know at some point or, if they don't, they will speculate about, and usually their speculation will be much worse than reality. Secrets lead to stress and anxiety.

If you are at a meeting and discussing changing parking arrangements, and at the conclusion the chair says, "Let's not share this information until we come up with some solid policies, so we don't get people riled up," you already know what is going to happen. Ultimately, someone tells someone else, or an agenda is left around and someone sees the items and draws conclusions. Soon the gossip around the water cooler is that parking fees are going up 35 percent, or there will only be parking for those in leadership positions, and everyone is needlessly angry and distressed.

Keep Employees Informed

Wouldn't it have been easier to let everyone in the company know that parking was discussed and here is what is happening so far? "We are going to put together a committee to look at other options; we are researching what other organizations do, and no conclusions have been made yet. We will keep you updated and if you have questions, ask your manager." Then staff don't waste valuable company time in useless speculation.

The first time I ran into a "no secrets" philosophy, I was suspicious. A boss I had come to respect arrived in my office to discuss an upcoming press conference and left my office door open. I was initially uncomfortable, thinking everyone could hear what we were discussing.

Remove The Guess Work

Over time, I saw how open communication works. No one was guessing about what was happening and they weren't even very interested, because if they wanted an answer, they knew it would be answered if they asked.

With few secrets, everyone from the caretakers to the chief financial officer felt part of the team. They knew what was going on, or knew they only had to ask their manager or our CEO to find out. It cut out so much wasted time on speculation. There just wasn't much fodder for the gossip wheel.

The next time you think something has to be kept a secret, ask yourself, "Does it, really?"

Whether people do this consciously or unconsciously, one reason people keep secrets is to exert power over someone else

– that whole "I am more important than you because I know something you don't know" type of thinking. Stop it!

Trying to keep secrets within a large organization, or a family for that matter, usually results in hurt feelings, miscommunication, and wasted time. If you really think about it, what is the point? Keeping secrets is exhausting.

Got It?

1. When decisions have not been reached, what parts of the information can be shared to alleviate fear or speculation? "I can't give specifics yet, what I can say is that . . ."

2. Before you say, "Don't' tell anyone," ask yourself why.

3. If you want to keep something a secret, then do. Don't share it with anyone.

Chapter 19

Take A Break!

When I was director of communications at United Way of Calgary, one of my young staff members gave me a bottle of the herb ginkgo biloba for my fiftieth birthday. It's said to improve memory.

While given in jest, I also knew that I wasn't remembering things the way I used to. I would catch myself frantically searching for my newly acquired reading glasses (they were on top of my head) or trying to remember who said what at meetings. I began to carry around a blank book to make accurate records of what was agreed on at the many meetings.

I'd have fleeting, worrying thoughts about what would happen in another few years if I needed such tangible aides at fifty. Luckily, the frenetic pace didn't give me many moments in which to worry. When one job was complete, three more were due, volunteers needed to be updated, and staff required support. Life was busy. I was sleeping six hours a night.

Weekly Time Out

As part of a leadership team professional development work-shop, the wise facilitators challenged us to book time off, prefer-ably a half day each work week, to do something for ourselves – take a walk, sit by a rushing mountain stream, read a profes-sional book, relax at the spa.

If, at your break time, they said, there is still something im-portant to do, write it down, then clear you mind and allow your-self to focus on the moment. "Ah," I thought, "that will only add to my stress when I face the even bigger workload accumulated during my time off."

Of a team of twelve, only one had a scheduled break. She went to a coffee shop every Friday morning to catch up on pro-fessional reading. She guarded that time carefully and I always respected her choice. She still accomplished lots at work and to this day maintains a healthy work-life balance.

Unfortunately, I had become so immersed in the day-to-day happenings that I rarely gave myself permission to take time to think, to do any professional reading, and, worst of all, to com-municate with myself. I never even asked myself why I kept such a hectic pace, or if something could be moved to anoth-er day, done differently, or not done at all. No one told me I couldn't take time to think. It was I who made the decision to plough through. What a huge mistake!

A few months later, I left United Way and went back to run-ning my own consulting company. I began to decompress. As time passed, my decision-making skills improved. While I've always been able to laugh, laughter came more easily. My mem-ory also returned.

It Wasn't The Boss

At first I thought this was because I had more control of my life. That was not true. The demands and the decisions regarding the work at United Way were always under my control. I could have blocked off time each week; I could have made time to take a walk most days. I could have spoken up and said, "I have this, this, and this to do; what is your priority?" and then let my boss make the decision how to allot my energies. My boss wasn't holding me hostage; I was.

Time Expands

Write a to-do list for the day, and beside each item, put the time you think it should take. Once your list is complete, add up the minutes and see if the total is more than an eight-hour day. If it is, move an item to another day. This strategy helped me tremendously not to set impossible goals.

If I think an article will take an hour, that's the time it will take. When sixty minutes are up, I try to be done. Before, I would work on something all day and then wonder where the time had gone. I also schedule times for looking at emails and returning phone calls. When I write down time limits, I become more efficient.

Have you ever had a short deadline thrown at you? Most times, you will meet it and come out with a good product. You simply change your expectations and prioritize your work. You do the same thing when you set your own time limits. You are much less likely to say, "Well, since I'm coming in on Saturday, I'll take the time to visit with Joan," or, "Oh, well; I'll go to that meeting even though I'm not really needed because I'm coming in on Saturday." Keep your head down, bum up, and focus!

Recently, I was chatting with a good friend who was concerned that she was losing her memory. I asked if she ever blocked out time to communicate with herself in a quiet place. She looked shocked – how could she, with so many responsibilities? She has children and aging parents to care for, a business to run, and friends to see. I told her my story. She said she would give it a try. Within a month she reported that her memory was improving and she was accomplishing more.

Are You Acting Like A Nutty Squirrel?

Breaks aren't a luxury for me any more. They are an important part of my routine. The pile on my desk looks less daunting after a long walk or a massage.

When you take time to build a relationship with yourself by communicating regularly about what is important, where you are going, who is going with you, and why, you will find yourself making more thoughtful choices, and being better able to focus on priorities. You will begin to feel less frustrated and disheartened and more confident in your decisions . . . and a lot less like a squirrel on drugs.

If you want to improve your memory, to become more efficient, and to feel clearer-headed and ready to act, take time to communicate with yourself weekly. You are worth it!

Got It?

1. What are three things you love to do and that you find invigorating or relaxing?

2. When did you last do any of those three things?

3. Look at your Day-Timer and mark off at least two hours per week to do something just for you. Half a day is better.

4. At the end of each day, make your to do list for the next day. Put a time limit beside each item and then check to ensure you don't have more hours than humanly possible. If you do, move items to the next day.

Chapter 20

Box Up Your Worries

Worry wastes enormous amounts of time. Think about a worry you have and, here and now, decide if it is something you can change. If it is, look for ways to change it. If not, focus on what you can do and accept what you can't.

Instead of letting worries infiltrate your thoughts all day long, sit down now and decide when in your day you are going to book a "worry time." Whether it is six in the morning, noon, or eight at night, when a worry pops into your head, say, "I will not deal with that now; I will deal with it at my worry time." And put it out of your mind.

I first read about booking a worry time in Robyn Sharma's book, *Who Will Cry When You Die?* He talked about all the useless time we spend jumbling our mind with worries. We often miss what is happening in the here and now because we are back in the past, or way off in the future; and who can control either?

Set A Schedule

I set a worry time and I stick to it conscientiously. My worry time is eight p.m. and so if I am writing, and all of a sudden I think, "What if this is useless information and people who buy the book want their money back?" I say, "Joan, you can't think about that right now; keep going. You can worry about that tonight at eight," and return to work.

If I am driving and I begin to relive a trauma at work or home, I admonish myself with, "Joan, enjoy the drive and worry about that tonight at eight." After I started this, I soon found I was taking pleasure in many things that previously simply happened, like making dinner or watching the buds turn into leaves on the trees. I began to feel more content and less stressed. I wasn't constantly thinking about everything that might, could, or had gone wrong.

At first, when eight p.m. came, I would relive the many unhappy and troublesome thoughts as I opened my "mental worry box." Sometimes, when eight p.m. came, I couldn't remember what it was I was going to worry about. I chalked it up to being over fifty, so rather than worry that I would forget, I kept (and still do) a small notepad in my purse to jot them down. Once written down, I don't have to keep trying to recall that worrying thought.

Be Kind To Your Mind

Some researchers say it takes twenty-one days to break a habit, so I worked on this, and after a couple of months, I began to realize that I was no longer having as many draining thoughts that used to take up a good part of my waking hours. The worry time was working!

When you think about it, if you are beating yourself up about something that happened in the past and you have absolutely no way to remedy the situation, it is exhausting. If you are "awfulizing" an upcoming event in your life; you are predicting failure before it even happens.

Olympic athletics visualize winning before an event, and it is a proven strategy for success. If you are visualizing a catastrophe, or failure, or a conflict, it is much more likely to happen. Stop this worthless and energy-draining behavior today.

Is all worry bad? No. In some cases, worry can help prepare you for an upcoming event or opportunity not being as great as you expect. It may cause you to think before you leap. Constant and unrealistic worry is what harms you.

Flick It Away

Another technique that works well is to think about a worry and then literally brush off both your shoulders and say, "Be gone." The physical act of brushing worry away really helps. Every time the worry pops into your head, say, "Be gone," and concentrate on whatever you are doing. Don't let something you have absolutely no control over control you.

You are the only one who can control your thoughts. Take control of what you are able to change and let the rest go. Rid yourself of worry. You will enjoy your life much more.

Got It?

1. Catch yourself worrying today and immediately stop and say, "I will worry about this at my worry time."

2. List all your worries and then go through each one and ask:
   - Can it or will it change? If you have no control over changing it, cross it off your list; if you can change it, write out a plan.
   - Some people even write a worry on a piece of paper and toss it in the garbage, flush it down the toilet, or burn it. The literal act of disposing of it helps.

3. Listen and see if you are passing your worries on to others. Ask yourself why. Will it help or hurt? Will you unconsciously be putting pressure on another? Think before you share your worries.

Chapter 21

Quit Complaining: Your Problems Will Diminish

Promise yourself today that for the next twenty-four hours you will not utter a single complaint or excuse. Do you think you can do it? I'll be surprised if you succeed. Few people go through a day without uttering some complaints or make some excuses. It takes practice to change, and I challenge you to begin today to make "no complaining" and "no excuses'" a habit.

Words are powerful and only you have the power to change your life by accepting that your choice of words dictates what kind of experience each day will be. Choose your words carefully.

One of my best friends, Nancy, lived her life complaint-free. In the more than forty years we were friends, I never heard her complain about her health. She achieved a university degree, worked full time at a government agency, was a single mom, had significant, chronic health challenges, and at some points spent months in hospital. Yet whenever I asked how she was doing, the answer was always, "I'm okay." Even when she was in intensive care.

She never *should haved* or *can't becaused* on herself. Instead, she embraced life with gusto and enjoyed her family and friends unconditionally. Her personal philosophy must have been, "Live the life you have to the fullest with no regrets."

When she was seventeen, Nancy was in a car accident that left her unable to use her legs and with little strength in her hands or movement in arms, and yet she would wheel her own chair, feed herself, and any toddler would soon be in her lap. Nancy would lean over, hook her arm around them, and boost them up. My kids loved to perch on her knee and hear a story, play a game, or have a chat. She always had time for children.

Refrain And Then Reframe

What's your first thought when something unpleasant happens to you? If it's, "I don't get paid enough to put up with this crap," or "Why do bad things always happen to me?" I'd say your beliefs are probably sabotaging you rather than helping you out.

How can you reframe your thoughts and comments? Adopt a new personal philosophy. While you may not have actually articulated it, most of us already have one. It's that little voice that helps us through the rough spots, or for some, pulls us even deeper into our personal pity party.

Some positive philosophies might include: "Blessed are the flexible for they shall not be bent out of shape." "In the scheme of things, will this matter in five minutes, five hours or five months?" "This too shall pass." "Make sure the idiot you are having an argument with isn't doing the same thing!" "Don't sweat the small stuff and everything is small stuff."

Take time to come up with one that works for you. Post it where you can see it and review it often because personal philosophies can change with time.

Start Afresh

Before you get out of bed tomorrow morning, tell yourself what a great day it will be. There will be lessons learned and people to see, food to taste and places to go. Aren't you lucky to be alive? And smile. Crease those cheeks!

Throughout your day, think about how lucky you are to be experiencing whatever it is you are experiencing. Be on the lookout for at least two people to compliment and, as you end your work day, write down three things that went well. Make this the last thing you do before heading home.

Whether you catch a bus or drive, concentrate on what is happening around you, enjoy it, and push any negative thoughts out of your head. Aren't you lucky to be alive?

Rather than articulating a litany of complaints tonight, talk about what went right. Look for ways to encourage those around you and to use words that are positive. If a difficult situation arose that you want to share, make sure you do not exaggerate; stick to facts and then comment on what you have learned. Once told, leave it and carry on.

Life is too short to waste your time worrying, *shoulding* yourself and others, or failing to enjoy the moment because you are caught in the past. Think before you speak, listen much more than you talk, and rid your vocabulary of negative words.

You've got one life to live, one mark to leave; why not leave a smile and a kind word? Adopting a personal philosophy will help. As people approach the end of their lives, one of their biggest concerns is what memories they will leave. Only you control the legacy you leave the world. Positive memories begin when communication is planned and positive.

Got It?

1. Listen to your words and do not allow any complaints or excuses to pass your lips.

2. Bring together your work team or a group of friends and come up with some personal philosophies. Choose one that resonates with you and post it in a visible place.

3. At the conclusion of each workday, think of three things that went well. Write them down.

4. Before you fall asleep, list three things that went well.

5. When you wake up in the morning, make your first action a smile.

LaVergne, TN USA
08 March 2011
219175LV00002B/1/P